· THE PITKIN GUIDE TO ·

TITANIC

Roger Cartwrig

THE ROYAL MAIL STEAMER *TITANIC* ranks with HMS *Victory*, the *Golden Hind* and the *Santa Maria* as one of the most famous ships in history. *Titanic*'s commercial career lasted just a few days in April 1912 but her legacy has remained strong throughout the 20th century and continues to enthral in the 21st century.

More than 22 million passengers entered the United States through Ellis Island and the port of New York between 1892 and 1924. Many of them were emigrants escaping the poverty and oppression of the Old World for the promise of the 'American Dream'.

When *Titanic* began her sea trials on 1 April 1912 she was the largest moving object ever made by man. She left Southampton for her maiden voyage on 10 April 1912, calling at Cherbourg before sailing on to Queenstown (now renamed Cobh) in Ireland. By the time she left Queenstown on 11 April she had on board 884 crew, 337 First Class, 271 Second Class and 706 Third Class (previously known as steerage) passengers, though, incredible as it may seem, different records give slightly different numbers – this was, after all, long before the days of computerized ticketing. The British inquiry gave the number of steerage passengers as 706 whilst at least one passenger list gave 712 and another 699.

Titanic was not full as a coal strike in Britain had caused many to cancel or postpone their trip. But the majority of those who boarded were fated not to arrive. Although different authorities reported numbers saved as between 705 and 803, what is clear is that around 1,500 lives – the rich, the poor, male, female, young and old, passengers and crew – were to perish in the icy waters of the North Atlantic on 15 April in what has become one of most famous and poignant shipping disasters the world has ever known.

What happened on that fateful voyage, and why were so many lost? Was it fate, bad luck, incompetence, sheer negligence – or a fatal combination of events?

RIGHT To wear the badge of a steward in First Class was a mark of distinction in the shipping industry.

THE NORTH ATLANTIC PASSENGER TRADE

B Y THE BEGINNING of the 20th century the steam-powered passenger ship had developed to a point where it was relatively safe and quite inexpensive for ordinary people to venture onto the wide ocean for a voyage. Whereas it could take weeks to cross the Atlantic in the middle of the 19th century, by 1900 the fastest ships were making the crossing from Europe to America in 5½ days, in considerable safety and comfort – opulent in First Class, very comfortable in Second Class and perfectly acceptable in Third Class/steerage. Indeed it was the Third Class boom in emigration to the USA and Canada that fuelled the expansion of the passenger trade across the North Atlantic and led to the building of huge (for the time) liners such as Titanic.

Competition on the North Atlantic was fierce. The main rivals were Britain's Cunard Line and White Star Line, and the German Nord Deutsche Lloyd (NDL) and Hamburg Amerika Line (HAPAG). By 1907 White Star had the largest and fastest passenger ships in the world – the big four – Adriatic, Baltic, Cedric and Celtic. Each was over 20,000 GRT (Gross Registered Tonnage), carried more than 2,800 passengers (the majority in Third Class/ steerage) and travelled at around 17 knots.

In the USA, the financier J. Pierpoint Morgan was eyeing the transatlantic passenger trade with a view to expanding his transportation and steel empire. He acquired a number of British and Belgian shipping companies and 51 per cent of the two big German concerns, NDL and HAPAG. He acquired the jewel in the crown of his International Mercantile Marine (IMM) when Lord Pirrie of Harland and Wolff assisted his acquisition of White Star from J. Bruce Ismay, son of the line's founder. Ismay remained in charge and also became chairman of IMM. Titanic may have been built and registered in Britain and have had a British crew, but she was paid for and owned by an American company.

Morgan also tried to acquire Cunard but was blocked by the British government, which aided Cunard with a subsidy to build two huge and fast liners which would be both record breakers and naval auxiliaries if war should break out. Both the Lusitania and Mauretania of 1907 were over 31,000 GRT and could travel at a rate of over 25 knots with more than 2,300 passengers. But how would White Star respond and compete?

BELOW White Star Line produced a commemorative brochure about their 'superliners', *Olympic* and *Titanic*; the ship shown on its cover is *Olympic*.

RIGHT The bust of Harland and Wolff chairman Lord Pirrie outside Belfast City Hall.

NAUTICAL MEASUREMENTS
One nautical mile = 6,080 feet or 1.15 land mile/1.85km
One knot = 1.15 land mile/1.85km per hour

BUILDING TITANIC AND HER SISTERS

C UNARD'S *LUSITANIA* and *Mauretania* owed their speed to the use of the recently developed steam turbine, replacing the more traditional triple expansion steam engines. This was an expensive option that White Star decided not to compete with. It was better, both White Star and Harland and Wolff argued, to build slightly slower but larger and even more luxurious vessels.

Lusitania and *Mauretania* were luxurious but the vessels that White Star and Harland and Wolff sketched out during a meeting between Ismay and Pirrie in 1907 were bigger and just as well-appointed. They decided on a trio of ships: 46,000 GRT and known as the 'Olympic class'. Let Cunard have the record of the two fastest liners: White Star would have the three biggest. As it transpired, the Olympic class liners were designed for 22.5 knots maximum speed (21 knots service speed). Rather than the four main turbines of the Cunarders driving four propellers, the Olympics would have two traditional engines and one turbine driving three propellers.

The design of the ships was begun by the chief designer at Harland and Wolff, the Honourable Alexander Carlisle, brother-in-law to Lord Pirrie, the chairman. After Carlisle retired in 1910, his position was taken by his assistant, Thomas Andrews, Pirrie's nephew.

The ships were designed with the latest safety measures. Electrically operated watertight doors, controlled from the bridge, were fitted to seal off supposedly watertight compartments. Without a watertight deck above the compartments, if too much water entered the forward compartments they would sink lower in the sea and the water would flow over the top and start filling up the next compartment. Nobody ever said the ship was unsinkable. An article by journalist Philip Gibbs before the maiden voyage said that the safety measures made her 'practically unsinkable'.

Within minutes of hitting the iceberg, Thomas Andrews, who lost his life that night, inspected the forepart of the ship and realized the flaw – the ship was going to founder.

THE WATERTIGHT COMPARTMENTS

Watertight compartments were one of the latest safety devices to be introduced. The concept of steel bulkheads that could hold back water had been proved when the Guion Line's *Arizona* hit an iceberg head on in November 1879 and survived. The bow crumpled but the bulkhead remained firm and watertight. It is impractical to have totally sealed bulkheads in a liner as the crew need to move to and fro, and thus a system of watertight doors was devised. The Olympic class could close the watertight doors very quickly. *Titanic* had 15 watertight bulkheads and theoretically she could float with two adjacent compartments flooded. After all, the designers pondered, what disaster would flood more than two adjacent compartments?

To be completely watertight the bulkheads needed to extend from the top of the ship's double bottom up to a steel main deck (see Diagram A). However, some of the bulkheads only extended upwards two or tree decks and there was no steel lid (see Diagram B).

BELOW The letters on the diagrams indicate the boat decks; O stands for 'orlop', the lowest deck of a ship. The thick vertical lines indicate watertight bulkheads; the thick horizontal line (Diagram A) indicates a steel watertight deck.

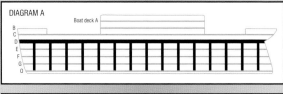

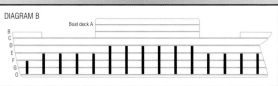

Building Titanic and Her Sisters

ABOVE The house-flag of the White Star Line.

BELOW Thomas Andrews, designer of *Titanic*, inherited the initial designs from the Honourable Alexander Carlisle after Carlisle retired.

Building a ship in the 1900s was a labour-intensive enterprise. Firstly there was the keel, an immense girder running alongside the bottom centreline of the ship. There was then a double bottom of between 5 feet 3 inches (1.6m) and 6 feet 3 inches (1.9m) deep. Divided into 44 watertight compartments, the double bottom served as both a storage area for water and as a safety feature. If the outer bottom was breached, the inner part of the double bottom should prevent water entering the hull proper.

To the skeleton of frames were affixed the plates, most around 30 feet (9m) long and 6 feet (1.8m) wide and around 1 inch (2.5cm) thick. The various joints were made using over three million rivets. The hull was made of steel plate, not the high tensile steel we know today. It was at its most brittle at the freezing point of water. Builders were beginning to switch from iron rivets to stronger steel ones: Harland and Wolff used a mixture of both.

Olympic, the first of the Olympic class trio, was launched on 20 October 1910, while the hull of *Titanic* was still a work in progress. *Olympic's* sea trials took place on 29 May 1911. Two days later *Titanic* was launched – the same day *Olympic* left Belfast: a clever piece of public relations. The third ship was not completed until 1914; she was to have been named *Gigantic* but was rechristened *Britannic* following the loss of *Titanic*.

It was not company policy to have lavish launching ceremonies so *Titanic* was never 'christened' with champagne in the traditional way. J.P. Morgan, whose money had paid for the ship, was present, however.

Once launched, *Titanic* was moved to the Thompson Graving Dock for fitting out. Her engines were installed; coal bunkers and boilers fitted; her rudder affixed to the graceful stern. Many have said that although her rudder was large, if it had been bigger still it might have enabled her to steer past the iceberg. Cabins and public spaces were prepared and her four funnels added to the superstructure. Only three funnels were operational; the fourth, being a dummy, was added for aesthetic reasons. In 1912 four funnels was the fashion for a crack Atlantic liner: *Mauretania* and *Lusitania* had four (functioning) funnels so the Olympics had to have four as well.

The Olympic class may not have been as fast as the record-breaking Cunarders but in terms of interior decor they were at least their equal. The design of the interiors on the Olympic class was mainly the work of Aldam Heaton & Co. Heaton established a partnership with Richard Norman Shaw, a well-known designer of country house interiors. The Edwardian style for an ocean liner followed land-based ideas in order to convince passengers that they were not actually at sea. The main staircase was a copy of the one in Belfast City Hall; Bruce Ismay is said to have seen it and remarked that one like it would be good for *Titanic*.

No expense was spared, especially in First Class where the public areas were very opulent indeed, with the finest woods and fabrics used throughout. The gallery-style entrance hall on the boat deck looked down onto the magnificent staircase and a Steinway grand piano. In the centre of the oval dome overhead, which flooded the area with natural light, was a 50-bulb dome chandelier, specially commissioned for Titanic. Those rich enough to afford First Class had a luxurious restaurant and a Ritz Carlton Grill. The wealthy also had their own lounge, panelled in oak with finely carved decoration, a grey marble fireplace, glazed mahogany bookcase and Louis XV-style clock. The room was carpeted in green and gold, a colourway that followed through in the furnishings, including 78 chairs and 15 settees grouped around low tables where afternoon tea and after-dinner coffee were served. First Class passengers also enjoyed a comfortable reading/writing room, plus sea-view Palm Courts on both sides of the ship, where light refreshments could be taken; these areas were in the style of an English gazebo, with cane furniture and ivy-trellised decor. There was a smoking room for gentlemen in First Class and a separate room for the ladies, mirroring the custom of the time that ladies retired after dinner for conversation whilst the men indulged in brandy and cigars. Those so inclined had the use of a squash racquets court, a gymnasium with a Turkish bath (men and women being allocated different times for its use), and a small heated swimming pool, filled with salt water, for which

passengers were charged 4s (20p). There were even lifts – three in First Class and one in Second.

Both First and Second Class had separate promenades along the boat deck. Second Class public rooms were similar to First Class, if more modest, but they had their library, smoking room and lounges. Third Class had simple public rooms (wooden floors, and white walls and ceilings) for relaxing and dining, plus a promenade and deck area at the stern. Poorer emigrants in particular were astonished to have the luxury of electric lighting, flushing toilets and regular meals – with waiter service – served on tables with linen cloths.

The completed Titanic was just over 46,000 GRT, 882 feet (268m) long, 92 feet (28m) wide and had a draught (the depth of water needed to float a ship) of 34 feet (10m). She had 29 boilers with 159 furnaces and was designed for a service speed of 21 knots. When full Titanic could carry 905 First Class, 564 Second Class and 1,134 Third Class passengers with 884 crew.

Financially, she was built on the basis whereby White Star would pay Harland and Wolff the actual construction costs plus 5 per cent

ABOVE LEFT Third Class passengers had their own smoking room at the stern, seen here in this replica.

ABOVE RIGHT The main staircase in First Class on *Titanic*, believed to be based on that in Belfast City Hall.

BELOW An invitation to the launch of RMS *Titanic* at the Harland and Wolff yard, Belfast, 31 May 1911.

Launch
OF
White Star Royal Mail Triple-Screw Steamer
"TITANIC"
At BELFAST,
Wednesday, 31st May, 1911, at 12·15 p.m.
Admit Bearer.

ABOVE *Titanic* on the slipway at the Harland and Wolff yard, just prior to her launch in May 1911.

(later *Britannic*), which was sunk during the First World War.

Harland and Wolff employed mainly Protestants; this was 1912 and Northern Irish politics and society were very divided. With the exception of the managers, most of the workforce lived around the yard in row after row of terraced houses. At the time the company was the major employer in Belfast, employing over 40,000 men. Skilled shipyard workers who built *Titanic* earned £2 per week (the equivalent of around £170 today); unskilled workers earned £1 or less per week. A group of craftsmen, led by Thomas Andrews, was to accompany *Titanic* on her maiden voyage. One of the group did not travel – but of those who did, none survived.

The ships became known individually as 'The Loved' (*Olympic*), 'The Damned' (*Titanic*) and 'The Forgotten' (*Britannic*). Belfast was proud of them, and the loss of *Titanic* was felt keenly here.

Although *Titanic* was inspected by the Board of Trade over 2,000 times during the course of her building, her sea trials lasted just one day – April Fool's Day 1912. A measured nautical mile was run off the Ulster coast and her systems were checked. Captain Edward Smith, the Commodore of the White Star Line, signed for the ship and she was handed over by the builders.

commission – the builder's profit was guaranteed. She cost £1.5 million but was only insured for £1 million – White Star carried the highest portion of insurance liability of the major shipping companies.

Titanic was laid down (the first stage in the construction of a ship, when building the keel, or bottom of the ship, is started on the slipway) on 31 March 1909 and she was launched on 31 May 1911. Her fitting out and sea trials lasted until 1 April 1912. Once the slipway was clear, work began on the third sister ship – *Gigantic*

ABOVE A mural of ship workers in Belfast; these were the men who built the famous ship.

RIGHT *Titanic* sails on her single day of sea trials.

PASSENGERS AND CREW

B Y 10 APRIL 1912, Titanic had a full complement of crew. Captain E.J. Smith (see panel) rejoined the ship from his Southampton home. Also joining was his previous Chief Officer from the Olympic, Henry Wilde. Wilde's arrival meant that the other officers on Titanic had to take a step down in rank – William Murdoch, who had been appointed as Chief Officer, was relegated to First Officer. The officers were joined by seamen, stokers, stewards, stewardesses, cooks, carpenters – the full range of skilled workers you would expect to find in a town, albeit a floating one.

The majority of the passengers joined at Southampton, with a small number joining at Cherbourg and Queenstown. Many First and Second Class came by boat-train, including the richest man in the world, John Jacob Astor, and his young wife, who had married the previous September. Some Third Class passengers had begun their journeys in Central Europe and it had been a long haul to Southampton. J. Pierpoint Morgan should have sailed but he was ill and his suite was given to a US store owner, Emil Brandis, who did not survive. Bruce Ismay, as chairman of White Star and IMM, was listed as an ordinary passenger. Lord Pirrie of Harland and Wolff should have sailed but his doctor advised that the voyage would be bad for his health.

Joining Astor in First Class was a cross-section of British and North American members of the upper classes: American businessman Benjamin Guggenheim was travelling in First Class with his valet; so too were Isidor Straus (the owner of Macy's department store in New York) and his wife Ida. Also travelling was the heir to the Widener tramway fortune, 27-year-old

CAPTAIN E.J. SMITH

Captain Edward John Smith was born in Stoke-on-Trent in 1850. At the tender age of 13 he went to Liverpool to begin a seafaring career, learning his craft on various sailing ships.

Smith joined White Star in 1880 as the Fourth Officer of the Celtic, and in 1887 received his first White Star command, the liner Republic. He gained a reputation amongst passengers and crew for quiet flamboyance and eventually became the Commodore, or Senior Captain, of the company. In this role he always commanded the newest and biggest ship on her maiden voyage. Such was his reputation as a seaman that some passengers would only cross the Atlantic in a ship commanded by him. By 1912 he was also a Commander in the Royal Naval Reserve (RNR); Smith's ships had the distinction of being able to wear the Blue Ensign of the RNR, rather than the traditional British Merchant Marine Red Ensign – which is why paintings of Titanic show a blue, rather than red, flag at the stern.

On 20 September 1911, under Smith's command, a major mishap occurred when Olympic collided with the cruiser HMS Hawke. Although the collision left two of Olympic's compartments flooded and one of her propeller shafts twisted, she was able to limp back to Southampton. On the bridge during this incident were Captain Smith and a local pilot. This was a financial disaster for White Star: the ship had to return to Belfast for repairs and, for speed, Harland and Wolff was forced to delay Titanic's completion as one of her propeller shafts and other parts had to be used to repair Olympic. This delayed Titanic's maiden voyage by nearly three weeks: no delay, no iceberg, no disaster.

Despite the collision, Smith was appointed in command of Titanic. It was rumoured that he might retire after her maiden voyage.

ABOVE Captain Smith (seated left) and his senior officers pose for a photograph on the bridge of Titanic.

ABOVE The richest man in the world: John Jacob Astor, who died on *Titanic*, photographed with his 18-year-old wife, Madeline, who survived.

RIGHT Benjamin Guggenheim, one of the heirs of wealthy mining magnate Meyer Guggenheim, did not survive the disaster.

BELOW A First Class ticket issued to the Reverend J. Holden, vicar of St Paul's Church, Portman Square, London. His wife fell ill the day before the ship sailed and the ticket was never used.

York by First Class passengers interested in his work. Apparently, on seeking permission, his bishop radioed back 'get off that ship!', an order that was to save Browne's life.

The middle classes inhabited Second Class. One of the passengers who gained fame through his association with *Titanic* was a British schoolteacher, 34-year-old Lawrence Beesley. He was one of the first of the survivors into print with his book, *The Loss of the SS Titanic: Its Story and Its Lessons, By One of the Survivors*, published in great haste in June 1912.

The Hart family from Ilford in Essex, England, proved very unlucky. Owing to the coal strike, they were transferred to

Harry Widener, a renowned bibliophile, returning to the USA with his parents after a European trip. The estimated combined wealth of Astor, Guggenheim, Straus and Widener Senior was over £70 million, a huge sum in 1912.

Major Archibald Butt, an aide to US President William Howard Taft, was also sailing home on *Titanic*. The president sent the cruiser USS *Chester* to search for his body; it was unsuccessful.

Also in First Class was Father Browne, who had been sent by the Irish Church to assess the new vessel's suitability for emigrants. He was a keen photographer and during the run from Southampton to Queenstown was offered passage to New

WHITE STAR LINE

YOUR ATTENTION IS SPECIALLY DIRECTED TO THE CONDITIONS OF TRANSPORTATION IN THE ENCLOSED CONTRACT.

THE COMPANY'S LIABILITY FOR BAGGAGE IS STRICTLY LIMITED, BUT PASSENGERS CAN PROTECT THEMSELVES BY INSURANCE.

First-Class Passenger Ticket per Steamship —— *Titanic*

SAILING FROM —— 10/4 1912

THE COST TO TRAVEL

Like a modern cruise ship, the fares from Britain to America on *Titanic* varied considerably according to the class of travel:

First Class parlor suite	£870 (the best accommodation)
First Class (berth)	£30 (cheapest First Class)
Second Class	£12
Third Class	£3 to £8 (depending on number of berths in the cabin)

The most expensive First Class passage was 290 times more than the cheapest Third Class. In 1912, £3 (the equivalent of £260 today) was a significant sum for an emigrant.

Another child in Third Class was 19-month-old Sidney Goodwin, travelling with his family, believed to be originally from Wiltshire, and latterly London.

The 706 Third Class passengers came from all over Ireland, the rest of the UK, Scandinavia, Northern, Southern and Central Europe and even the near East. Fares were relatively cheap and it was the promise of a new life that drove them to the Americas. Of the 706, only 175 would live to see the New World.

Huge amounts of luggage came aboard. First Class passengers travelled with a large number of cases and steamer trunks. Many travelling Third Class had all their worldly possessions with them.

LEFT Millvina Dean with her mother and older brother. The baby was lowered in a basket from the sinking ship.

LEFT Sidney Goodwin, who perished with his siblings and parents on board *Titanic*.

BELOW Lawrence Beesley survived and wrote about his experiences, criticizing White Star Line.

Titanic from an older White Star ship, where they were booked to travel in First Class. Benjamin Hart, his wife Esther and family were emigrating to Winnipeg in Canada, where he planned to open a tobacconist shop. Eva Hart was just seven years old when she and her parents boarded *Titanic* as Second Class passengers, rather than First Class as intended – though on *Titanic* Second Class would have been just as opulent and comfortable as First Class on an older vessel.

Less is known about the steerage passengers, although it is from their ranks that the last survivor of *Titanic* came: Elizabeth Gladys Dean, better known as Millvina, whose family was emigrating.

SETTING SAIL

10 APRIL 1912: at 12 o'clock the bugler sounded the lunch signal. As the passengers filed to their meals, the ship's whistle sounded and *Titanic* left her berth – and nearly ran into disaster. As she approached the liners *Oceanic* and *New York*, which were crowded with sightseers, the surge of water ahead of *Titanic* and the weight of people aboard *New York* caused *New York*'s stern lines to part and she swung out into *Titanic*'s path. Quick thinking by a tug captain averted a collision. However, if the ships had met *Titanic*'s voyage would have been delayed.

Once clear of Southampton, Captain Smith set sail across the English Channel for Cherbourg, where *Titanic* anchored around sunset. The few passengers joining the ship were brought out by two tenders, one for First Class and another for Second/Third Class. Even though there were only a few passengers coming aboard, propriety had to be observed and First Class had to have their own tender.

ABOVE *Titanic* leaves Southampton at the start of her maiden voyage.

RIGHT Mrs Galvin of Queenstown was allowed to sell her wares to passengers leaving from the port. Here she waits while they board the tender that will take them out to *Titanic*.

BELOW *Titanic* anchored off Queenstown while mail and passengers were taken out to her by tender. A lucky few left the ship here – her last port of call.

Titanic headed for Queenstown, Ireland, her final stop before New York. At Queenstown, local tenders were used and seven passengers disembarked, among them Father Browne (as instructed by his bishop), who had used the opportunity to take photographs on board as he sailed from Southampton to Ireland, and a fireman, John Coffey, believed to have deserted ship.

A further seven Second Class and 130 Third Class passengers came aboard. As the ship left Queenstown, newly joined Eugene Daly in Third Class played *A Lament for Erin* on his bagpipes: he survived.

In the bowels of the ship, in temperatures of over 120 degrees Fahrenheit, an army of stokers known as the 'Black gang' fed the boilers with coal. One of the bunkers was actually on fire during the voyage, a fact that was not considered unusual at the time. Bruce Ismay and the Chief Engineer, Joseph Bell, discussed how to work the ship up to full speed. Those who spoke to them said they were aware that *Titanic* could not challenge the record. Nevertheless, Ismay clearly wanted to see what the ship could do.

LIFE ON BOARD

AS THE PASSENGERS settled down to their voyage, most appeared delighted with the standard of accommodation. The most sumptuous and expensive accommodation were two parlour suites on B Deck, which benefited from a spacious sitting room, two bedrooms, two wardrobe rooms, a bathroom and lavatory, plus a 48-feet (14.5-m) long private promenade. The sitting rooms were panelled in walnut and sycamore, with a carved ceiling and parquet floor with a large rug; the furniture was mahogany and there was a fireplace for electric heat, plus additional radiators; ceiling lights were covered with beaded glass lampshades and other lamps had silk shades. Bedrooms were fully carpeted and there were two ornate brass bedsteads; other bedroom furniture was of mahogany, including the washstand cabinet which was topped with marble. Hanging rails in the wardrobes held lifebelts. The bathroom (shared between the two bedrooms) consisted of an enamelled rolled-edge bath with shower enclosure, and a basin with veined marble surround and marble-framed mirror above. The Doulton lavatory was situated in its own compartment.

Typical Second Class staterooms were more simply furnished, though still in mahogany and extremely comfortable. There were bunks instead of individual bedsteads, and fold-up wash cabinets with a reservoir for water – piped running water was exclusive to First Class passengers. Second Class passengers shared public baths and lavatories.

Much of the space in Third Class was taken up with public latrines (one for women, two for men). Some cabins had sprung mattresses on mahogany bunks, a wall seat and washbasin. The cheapest rooms had iron bunks and there was no storage facility or washbasin; bedding was a straw-filled mattress with a cotton cover, and a blanket.

ABOVE The original plan was for *Titanic*'s lifeboats to be placed three abreast on the boat deck. White Star decided that this would impede passengers who wanted to stroll along the deck so the number of lifeboats was reduced.

FIRST CLASS STATEROOM

First Class passenger, American artist Francis David Millet, wrote a letter home describing his accommodation:

'The rooms … are larger than the ordinary hotel room and much more luxurious with wooden bedsteads, dressing tables, hot and cold water, etc., etc., electric fans, electric heater and all … I have the best room I have ever had in a ship and it isn't one of the best either … . No end of furniture, cupboards, wardrobe, dressing table, couch etc., etc.. Not a bit like going to sea.'

Many First Class passengers had their servants with them (accommodated in special inside cabins). First Class was highly formal: ladies might change five or six times a day, and every night on a voyage (barring the first and last) everyone dressed for dinner – the high point of the First Class experience.

Several First Class passengers sent and received 'Marconigrams'. Radio at sea (see page 20) was still a novelty and, despite the high cost, many frivolous messages were posted. The Marconi operation was a commercial one and priority was given to the wealthy passengers who paid 12s 6d (65p) for the first 10 words and 9d (4.5p)

ABOVE A replica of the comforts of a bedroom of a First Class suite.

LEFT An artist's impression of a Second Class stateroom on *Titanic*, more luxurious than First Class on many older vessels.

BELOW A replica of a four-berth Third Class cabin on board *Titanic*.

per word thereafter: the equivalent of £54 and £3.25 respectively today. At one point sending these messages actually interfered with receiving ice warnings. Nevertheless, over 250 passenger telegrams were sent and received during the voyage.

There was a band for First Class, led by Wallace Hartley from Colne in Lancashire, but apart from that, and betting on the ship's progress, there was little organized entertainment. First and Second Class

THE MENUS

FIRST CLASS
As well as standard breakfast fare – Quaker oats, kidneys and bacon, and omelettes cooked to order – there was a wide variety of other choices including baked apples, grilled mutton and lamb collops. Luncheon might consist of roast Surrey capon or chicken *à la* Maryland, or a buffet of lobster, galantine of chicken and corned ox tongue. To start, the dinner menu offered such delicacies as oysters or consommé Olga, with entrees of sauté of chicken lyonnaise, roast duckling with apple sauce or roast squab with cress, served with a choice of vegetables and chateau, parmentier or boiled new potatoes, with deserts of French ice cream, peaches in chartreuse jelly, apple meringue or Waldorf pudding.

SECOND CLASS
A typical lunch could be: pea soup, spaghetti au gratin, vegetable dumplings or cold cuts. For dinner: consommé or tapioca to start; baked haddock with a sharp sauce, curried chicken and rice, spring lamb or roast turkey as the main course; followed by wine jelly, American ice cream, assorted nuts, cheese and biscuits, plus coffee.

THIRD CLASS
Tea was served at every meal. Breakfast included porridge, ham and eggs. herrings, ling fish and egg sauce, fresh bread and butter. One o'clock dinner offered rice soup, roast beef with brown gravy and vegetables, followed by plum pudding with a sweet sauce or fruit. At teatime there were cold meats and pickles, stewed figs and rice. A supper of gruel, cabin biscuits and cheese was also available.

TRIPLE SCREW STEAMER "TITANIC."

2ND CLASS APRIL 14, 1912.

DINNER.

CONSOMMÉ TAPIOCA
BAKED HADDOCK, SHARP SAUCE
CURRIED CHICKEN & RICE
SPRING LAMB, MINT SAUCE
ROAST TURKEY, CRANBERRY SAUCE
GREEN PEAS   PURÉE TURNIPS
BOILED RICE
BOILED & ROAST POTATOES
PLUM PUDDING
COCOANUT SANDWICH
WINE JELLY   AMERICAN ICE CREAM
NUTS ASSORTED
FRESH FRUIT
CHEESE   BISCUITS
COFFEE

ABOVE Second Class dinner menu from the final meal on board *Titanic*. This menu was kept by survivor Mrs Bertha J. Marshall (née Watt).

RIGHT Wallace Hartley from Colne in Lancashire, *Titanic*'s bandleader. He and his musicians all perished as they played in an effort to bring comfort to those on the sinking vessel.

passengers (in their own areas, of course) promenaded, gossiped, drank, made business deals and gambled – there was at least one professional gambler on board. Apparently very few First Class passengers used the gym or Turkish bath – they were regarded as a gimmick. Down in Third Class, language and cultural differences were broken down with singing and dancing in the social halls.

The only routine was meals, which in post-Edwardian times were lavish by today's standards. First Class could dine in either the main dining saloon (which seated 550 and included the Captain's table with seating for six) or the à la carte restaurant; lunch and dinner were announced by a bugler, with a dress-call sounding half an hour earlier. Second Class meals were very acceptable, if less extravagant than in First Class; passengers were called to their dining saloon by a gong. Third Class offered good, wholesome fare in two dining saloons (one for single men, the other for women and families); long tables for 14 people were set up with menu cards for the whole day's meals, rather than individual ones for each meal as provided in First and Second Class.

To prepare the food were 16 cooks, 15 scullions, 14 bakers, seven butchers, plus extra cooks for the crew. There were no fewer than 324 stewards and 18 stewardesses (of whom 17 survived) to serve and look after the passengers in both the restaurants and the cabins. The separate Ritz Carlton Grill, for First Class passengers, employed 20 staff.

Amongst all this the crew went about their duties, ironing out any problems that occurred – of which there were very few. One thing that was not done was to hold a lifeboat drill: this was *Titanic* – what could possibly go wrong?

A FEAST OF FOOD

According to records, when *Titanic* set sail the comestibles and other consumables for the voyage included:

Fresh meat	75,000 lbs (34,000kg)
Fresh fish	11,000 lbs (5,000kg)
Salt and dried fish	4,000 lbs (1,800kg)
Bacon and ham	7,500 lbs (3,500kg)
Poultry and game	25,000 lbs (11,300kg)
Fresh eggs	40,000
Sausages	2,500 lbs (1,100kg)
Potatoes	40 tons
Onions	3,500 lbs (1,500kg)
Tomatoes	3,500 lbs (1,500kg)
Fresh asparagus	800 bundles
Fresh green peas	2,500 lbs (1,100kg)
Lettuce	7,000 heads
Sweetbreads	1,000 lbs (450kg)
Ice cream	1,750 lbs (800kg)
Coffee	2,200 lbs (1,000kg)
Tea	800 lbs (350kg)
Rice, dried beans, etc.	10,000 lbs (4,500kg)
Sugar	10,000 lbs (4,500kg)
Flour	250 barrels
Cereals	10,000 lbs (4,500kg)
Apples	36,000
Oranges	36,000
Lemons	16,000
Grapes	1,000 lbs (450kg)
Grapefruits	13,000
Jam and marmalade	1,120 lbs (500kg)
Fresh milk	1,500 gallons (5,500 litres)
Fresh cream	1,200 quarts (1,100 litres)
Condensed milk	600 gallons (2,300 litres)
Fresh butter	6,000 lbs (2,700kg)
Ale and stout	15,000 bottles
Wine	1,000 bottles
Spirits	850 bottles
Minerals	1,200 bottles
Cigars	8,000

BELOW Both *Olympic* and *Titanic* had a gymnasium with the latest keep-fit equipment of the day. Here an elegant female passenger tries out a 'cycle-racing machine'.

BOTTOM Elegant crockery of First Class, decorated with the White Star logo.

15

THE UNSINKABLE DREAM?

RIGHT *Titanic*'s lifeboats: had there been more, fewer lives would have been lost.

THE CATACOMB-LIKE nature of the large passenger ship is shown below in this cutaway diagram. The largest compartments are those for the engines and associated boilers and machinery. It is worth noting that the illustrator 'got it wrong': trunking is seen leading upward towards the first three funnels and (correctly) there is none leading to the fourth funnel – but there

Much of the crew accommodation was forward

The cranes (shown forward and aft) were for loading cargo and supplies

Bridge

The main staircases and lifts are shown between the first and second funnels

First Clas

BOILERS   COAL   BOILERS   COAL

Boilers

RIGHT Replica of *Titanic*'s radio room.

is smoke seen coming from it. The fourth funnel was a dummy and for aesthetic purposes only.

The labyrinth nature of the different levels of accommodation demonstrates how difficult it would have been for the Third Class passengers, housed mainly towards the stern, to find their way to the open decks as the ship's head slowly slipped beneath the waves.

FAR LEFT Replica sitting room of a First Class suite.

LEFT Engine room telegraph on the bridge, used to give orders to engineers deep in the bowels of the ship.

BELOW LEFT Replica of the ship's wheel that failed to produce a sharp enough turn to avoid the iceberg.

BELOW Engineers working in the boiler room, typical of an early 20th-century coal-fired ship.

Dummy funnel (incorrectly showing smoke)

The main staircases and lifts are shown between the third and fourth funnels

Second Class

The cranes (shown forward and aft) were for loading cargo and supplies

Third Class

The ship's double bottom

DISASTER IN THE NORTH ATLANTIC

O N THAT FATEFUL Sunday, 14 April, *Titanic* gradually worked up to around 22 knots. Captain Smith, as was part of his duties, inspected the ship with his officers that day and conducted a church service for First and Second Class passengers, who were allowed to mix at church.

During the afternoon it became increasingly colder. *Titanic* was approaching the southern edge of expected ice. Ice is very prevalent in the North Atlantic during April, as the bergs that have calved off the Greenland glaciers drift continually further south. Reports show that *Titanic* received ice warnings from other ships. Some First Class survivors recounted how Ismay showed them an ice warning he had received. Although Captain Smith did not slow down, he did take the ship slightly further south than usual in an attempt to avoid the ice.

As night fell, calm and starry but with a haze at sea level, Captain Smith ordered the temperature of the freshwater tanks be checked to ensure the water would not freeze. Second Officer Charles Lightoller, when he was relieved as officer of the watch by First Officer William McMaster Murdoch, said that he had ordered that all lights below the bridge be put out so

that the glare would not impair the men's vision; they knew they were in the vicinity of ice – they could smell it.

That night Smith dined with a group of First Class American passengers: Major Butt (President Taft's aide), Mr and Mrs Thayer, and Mr and Mrs Widener. The Wideners and Mrs Thayer survived, and Mrs Thayer testified that Captain Smith did not drink any alcohol that night and left early to visit the bridge.

The voyage was well into its final third, just 48 hours out of New York. By 11 p.m. most passengers were in bed. Some men remained in the First Class smoking room, talking and enjoying a nightcap.

Titanic continued through the night at about 22.5 knots. Around 11.30 p.m., high above the ship in the crow's nest, Fred Fleet (the single lookout) was peering into the icy darkness. He had no binoculars but in the haze saw a shape just 500 yards (500m) away. He immediately rang his bell to alert the bridge (there was no telephone) and yelled out, 'Iceberg dead ahead!' Murdoch acted instantly,

SPEEDING INTO DANGER

It was normal practice in the early part of the 20th century not to slow down for ice, or even fog. Only the great explorer Ernest Shackleton told the British inquiry that he would have reduced speed. Other captains said they would do what Smith did – pass through the danger as quickly as possible. The inquiry did state that in future ships should slow down near ice or fog. Recent reconstructions have shown that had *Titanic* been travelling at around 10 knots the collision could have been avoided, but it is easy to be wise after the event. Smith was exonerated of negligence.

ordering an emergency turn to port (left) and hit the switch to close the watertight doors. Quartermaster Robert Hitchens turned the wheel. If *Titanic* had had a bigger rudder she might have turned more quickly but as it was she scraped against an underwater protruding portion of a relatively small iceberg. It was too late. There was no big gash but it is believed that the rivets popped and the plates they held opened up along 300 feet (90m) of her hull. Six compartments opened; she could only float with no more than three compartments flooded.

Some of the crew felt a slight shudder; one thought that the ship had lost a propeller and would have to return to Belfast for repairs after New York. To the passengers nothing seemed amiss: Mrs Thayer, in her suite, felt just a slight jar; Martha Stevenson heard a grinding noise; Lawrence Beesley only felt an extra heave of the engines. The officers, however, were more concerned. Captain Smith rushed to the bridge and was apprised of the collision. Thomas Andrews went below to find water rushing in. It was then that he realized the fatal flaw. There was nothing to stop water in the compartments overflowing into each other – *Titanic* would founder that night. He told Smith and Ismay, who had joined him, the grim news. And grim news it was: there were over 2,200 souls on board and only 1,178

lifeboat spaces. With hindsight it is easy to say there were not enough lifeboats on the *Titanic* as planned and built. However, legally there were.

Smith knew his ship was doomed but was concerned to avoid panic. He ordered a distress message be sent out by the radio operators, Jack Phillips and Harold Bride. Initially they sent the usual CQD (Come Quick Distress) signal but then decided to use the newly adopted SOS. The messages were answered by a number of ships, including *Titanic*'s sister, *Olympic*. All were some distance away and unlikely to arrive within the two hours Thomas Andrews believed the ship might stay afloat.

Phillips and Bride kept transmitting for as long as they had power. It is reported that a crew member tried to steal Phillip's lifejacket but was restrained. Bride survived the disaster; Phillips did not.

ABOVE Recovered from the wreck: the bell that Fred Fleet rang to warn of the iceberg dead ahead.

LEFT Was this the iceberg that sank *Titanic*? Photographed from a passing ship a few days after the disaster, paint along the berg's waterline suggests that it may have been the culprit.

ABOVE *Date with Destiny*: this painting of *Titanic* and the fatal iceberg is by David Hoddinott.

Once the true scale of the disaster became apparent, Smith ordered that the passengers be led to the boat stations. There seems to have been little systematic planning. Stewards went from cabin to cabin (there was no PA system) and roused the passengers. Many were reluctant to leave their warm beds and in the concern to prevent panic little was done to hurry them up.

The crew seemed unsure of the procedures they should follow short of 'women and children first'. *Titanic's* lifeboats could be lowered fully loaded but the officers did not appear to be aware of this. Boats were partially filled,

RIGHT Jack Phillips in *Titanic's* radio room. It was from here that he and Harold Bride sent the CQD distress call followed by the first-ever use of SOS.

lowered and then more passengers were expected to climb down rope ladders to them, or else the boats would go to one of the gangway ports to fill up completely. This plan came to nothing. Lifeboat 7 was the first to be launched at 12.45 a.m. (65 minutes after hitting the iceberg). Although it was rated to hold 65 people it carried only 27; the crew were fearful of overloading the boats, and in any event anticipated them being used as ferries to take passengers to the safety of other ships in the vicinity.

Slowly the true magnitude of the disaster began to dawn on the passengers, especially when signal rockets started to be fired. John Jacob Astor placed his young wife in a boat and then waited calmly. Benjamin Guggenheim and his valet were in their nightclothes on the

boat deck. Guggenheim is reported to have suggested they go and change so that they could 'go down like gentlemen'.

Although later there was press speculation, it seems that there was no class distinction once passengers had reached the boat deck. However, Third Class were aft and lower down in the ship, and it took time for news of the evacuation to reach them. Many of the emigrants spoke little or no English and many wanted to take their possessions with them. The lifeboats themselves were positioned nearer to the First and Second Class areas. 'Women and children first' was adhered to, although some officers did let men into the boats if there were no women near by. Major Arthur Peuchen of the Canadian Militia had felt the collision as no more than a large wave hitting the ship. On the boat deck he saw a boat being lowered and offered his services as a yachtsman. He was told that if he was seaman enough to climb down a rope then he could go – and he survived.

According to the official casualty figures there were 109 children on board. Imagine the terror they faced. Many could not speak English and all around them were adults who were clearly distressed.

ABOVE Passengers congregate on deck wearing their lifejackets as they wait to enter the lifeboats under the direction of officers.

LOVE STORY

Isidor and Ida Straus were returning from a European trip. Isidor – the owner of Macy's department store – was reputed to be worth over £10 million. Both in their 80s, Isidor and Ida had been married for many years and were a devoted couple. Mrs Straus was placed in a lifeboat and asked if her husband could join her as a man of his age would stand no chance in the icy waters. It was agreed that he could – but he refused: if the other men were staying, so would he. Consequently, Mrs Straus climbed out of the lifeboat, telling the occupants that she and her husband had been together for over 50 years and that they would stay together now. They were last seen sitting on the promenade deck holding hands.

LEFT Isidor and Ida Straus, who died when *Titanic* sank.

Eva Hart was sleeping when *Titanic* struck the iceberg. Her father rushed into the cabin to alert Eva and her mother. Mrs Hart had felt uneasy about the ship and, fearing some catastrophe, slept during the day and stayed awake in her cabin at night, fully dressed. After wrapping Eva in a blanket, Benjamin Hart carried her to the deck. He placed his wife and daughter in Lifeboat 14 and told Eva to 'hold Mummy's hand and be a good girl'. It was the last thing her father ever said to her, and the last time she ever saw him.

Millvina Dean, just weeks old at the time of the disaster and the youngest child on board, was placed with her mother and brother in Lifeboat 10. Like Eva Hart, she survived but never saw her father again. When Millvina died in 2009 she was the last survivor of *Titanic*.

Of the 109, 52 children were lost – all from Third Class.

As half-filled lifeboats were lowered, many Third Class passengers were struggling to find the boat deck. Bruce Ismay is said to have gone from boat to boat, becoming increasingly concerned. He truly believed that all the women

ABOVE The lifeboats were placed high up on the ship and it was a slow and frightening descent for those in them.

TOP LEFT Eva Hart with her parents. Eva and her mother survived; her father did not.

TOP RIGHT Millvina Dean, seen here at a *Titanic* exhibition in 1994. The last survivor of the tragedy, she died aged 97.

SURVIVAL STATISTICS

Comparative survival rates amongst the classes are shocking.

	Women and Children	Men	Total
First Class	94 per cent	31 per cent	60 per cent
Second Class	81 per cent	10 per cent	44 per cent
Third Class	47 per cent	14 per cent	25 per cent
Crew	87 per cent	22 per cent	24 per cent

and children were off the ship, and asked an officer if he could get into a boat. The rumours that he dressed as a woman are unfounded. However, for the chairman of IMM to survive when nearly 1,500 died caused considerable adverse comment. Nevertheless, Ismay did leave *Titanic* in a lifeboat.

When the ship went down a few people were plucked from the ocean. However, as the water was near to freezing point, many died immediately on entering the waves, and many more died of hypothermia.

Of the navigation staff, only Second Officer Charles Lightoller, Fourth Officer Joseph Boxhall and Fifth Officer Harold Lowe survived to give an account of the disaster. Of the eight stewardesses, seven were rescued. All the senior

engineers lost their lives – they kept the lights on as long as possible in an effort to help others. Of the pursers, only two female clerks survived. The youngest crew member, a 14-year-old boy by the name of Watson, was working on *Titanic* as a bell boy for a monthly wage of £2. His body was never found.

THE BAND PLAYED ON

Wallace Hartley, leader of *Titanic*'s band, started to play as the evacuation began. He led his seven musician colleagues further and further aft as the waters engulfed the ship. They made no attempt to escape but continued to play to the hundreds of people trapped on the vessel once the last boat left. It is believed that the last piece they played was *Songe d'Automne* (not *Nearer My God To Thee* as is often quoted). None of the musicians survived. They are commemorated at Liverpool's Philharmonic Hall on a plaque that includes the inscription: 'Courage and compassion joined make the hero and the man complete.'

A SURVIVOR REMEMBERS

'The Titanic was all aglow with lights as if for a function. First we saw the lights of the lower deck snuffed out. A while later and the second deck illumination was extinguished in a similar manner. Then the third and upper decks were darkened, and without plunging or rocking the great ship disappeared slowly from the surface of the sea.'

James McGough, a 36-year-old buyer from Philadelphia

BELOW Her lights kept on by gallant engineers, *Titanic* begins her journey to the depths. An illustration based on the first-hand account of survivor Frederick Hoyt.

TO THE RESCUE

IT HAS LONG been claimed that those on *Titanic* saw the lights of a ship nearby – and it is assumed that ship was the *Californian*, which was stopped in the ice field. *Californian*'s captain, Stanley Lord, had reports of a large steamer that turned and sailed away, and of signal rockets. However, rockets were the means by which company ships without radio communicated with each other. *Californian*'s radio was shut down for the night.

Captain Lord always denied he was near *Titanic* and that it was another ship that the survivors reported. Lord was castigated by the British inquiry and spent the rest of his life trying to clear his name; he died in 1962.

If it was the *Californian* then all on board *Titanic* could have been saved before she sank, as no lives were lost in the actual collision between *Titanic* and the iceberg.

For years it was thought that a ship, presumably the *Californian*, was as little as 5 miles (8km) away. Recent evidence, based on the true position of the wreck of *Titanic*, suggests that this ship was as much as

BELOW One of the collapsible lifeboats makes its way towards the rescue ship.

VIOLET JESSOP

In 1910, at the age of 23, Violet Jessop became a stewardess on *Olympic*. She boarded *Titanic* as a stewardess on 10 April 1912. In her memoirs, Violet described how, after the collision, she was ordered up on deck where she watched as the crew loaded the lifeboats. She was later ordered into Lifeboat 16 and, as the boat was being lowered, one of the ship's officers gave her a baby to look after. The next morning Violet was rescued by *Carpathia*, along with the rest of the survivors. According to Violet, while on board *Carpathia* a woman grabbed the baby she was holding and ran off without saying a word.

Many years later Violet received an anonymous telephone call from someone stating that she was that baby, but there was no further contact and the identity of the child remains unknown.

ABOVE Violet Jessop: as well as surviving the *Titanic* disaster, in the First World War she was a nurse on *Britannic* and also survived the sinking of that ship, in the Aegean.

18 miles (29km) away; the unusual weather conditions that night caused the illusion of it appearing to be much closer.

And so it was the Cunard liner *Carpathia*, on her way to Europe, that picked up the SOS. Captain Arthur Rostron turned his ship around and headed for *Titanic*'s position. Passengers donated warm

LEFT Margaret (the Unsinkable Molly) Brown and Arthur Rostron, Captain of RMS *Carpathia*.

THE UNSINKABLE MOLLY BROWN

Margaret Brown from Colorado had married well, divorced and had become a well-educated woman. She was returning to the USA on *Titanic*. Margaret helped others board the lifeboats but was finally convinced to leave the ship in Lifeboat 6. Later she became known as 'The Unsinkable Molly Brown' by historians (although she never used the name Molly) because of her involvement in the ship's evacuation, taking an oar herself in her lifeboat and protesting for the men in the boat to go back to look for survivors. On board *Carpathia* she took a leadership role among the women passengers.

BELOW As the casualty lists appear outside the White Star offices in Southampton, the magnitude of the disaster becomes apparent to a shocked and disbelieving public.

clothing, hot drinks were prepared and, because of the danger of ice, extra lookouts were posted.

It was a long, cold night for those in the lifeboats. Survivor Mary Davis Wilburn reported: 'The dead came up holding children in their arms. The poor people never had a chance.' *Titanic* slipped beneath the waves at around 2.20 a.m. A great cry was heard by those in the boats, which had been rowed some way from the ship to avoid the suction as it went down. The funnels crashed, there was a rumble as the boilers broke free from their mountings – and then silence.

One heroine of the night was Margaret 'Molly' Brown (see panel); another was the Countess of Rothes, who took command of one of the lifeboats having declared the crew incompetent!

At dawn, *Carpathia* found the survivors – 705 weary souls. It was a sad sight as the ship steamed into New York a few days later. She had relayed survivors' lists and crowds were awaiting her arrival. All over the US, Canada and Britain anxious relatives and friends were scanning the casualty lists.

AFTERMATH: THE INQUIRIES

THE SURVIVORS arrived in New York on the evening of 18 April. The dead lay either on *Titanic* or in the sea.

No sooner had Bruce Ismay stepped off *Carpathia* than he was summoned to a Senate hearing chaired by Senator William Aulden Smith. As IMM was an American company, the Senator believed it was his right to hold an inquiry despite the *Titanic* being a British ship. The British government raised no objection and the inquiry started on 17 April. Senator Smith finished his 18-day inquiry on 25 May.

It was, perhaps, unfortunate that the British inquiry was held by the Board of Trade, the very body that had inspected and passed *Titanic*, and was to last twice as long as its American counterpart. Much comment was made in the press about the

lack of lifeboats although the provision complied with Board of Trade regulations. Nevertheless, within days of the tragedy ocean liners were carrying extra lifeboats so that there was a space for everybody.

In addition, despite Captain Smith's decision to speed into the ice field being established practice for the time, it was declared that in future such behaviour in fog or ice would be considered negligent. Smith was, however, exonerated. It was Captain Lord of the *Californian* who was castigated.

RIGHT In London a young newspaper seller displays the latest news of the sinking – ironically outside Oceanic House, the offices of White Star Line.

BELOW J. Bruce Ismay answers hostile questions at the US Inquiry chaired by Senator Smith.

EYEWITNESS ACCOUNT

Seaman Frank Evans, who went back to the wreckage to recover any survivors after *Titanic* sank, was a witness at the inquiry:

Evans: There were plenty of dead bodies about us.
Senator Smith. How many? Scores of them?
Evans: You couldn't count them, sir. I was afraid to look over the sides because it might break my nerves down.

RECOVERING THE LOST

WHILE THE INQUIRIES were taking place, many bodies were recovered, embalmed and, where identified, released to their families. John Jacob Astor's body was found still in his overcoat.

Canadian ships were involved in the terrible task of recovering the bodies, and most of the remains were taken to Halifax, Nova Scotia. Many of them are buried here in three cemeteries: 19 in Mount Olivet Catholic Cemetery; 10 in Baron de Hirsch Jewish Cemetery; and 121 in Fairview Lawn Cemetery, where the graves are laid out in the shape of a ship – including those of the 42 victims who remain unidentified. Details for those unidentified are recorded, for example:

Grave 328 Mt Olivet RC Cemetery

Four foot six inches. Age about 14, hair golden brown. Marks: very dark skin, refined features. Lace-trimmed red-black overdress, black underdress, green striped undershirt, black woollen shawl and felt slippers. Probably Third Class passenger.

THE UNKNOWN CHILD

Amongst the bodies collected by Halifax cable ship *Mackay Bennett* was that of a baby. The crew were so moved that they paid for a memorial to the 'The Unknown Child of the Titanic' in Fairview Lawn Cemetery. In 2002, DNA testing suggested that the child was Eino Viljami Panula, a member of a Finnish family. He was 13 months old when *Titanic* sank. His mother Maria and four brothers also drowned. Relatives arrived in Halifax to visit the grave, where they decided that the child's body should remain. However, further testing in 2007 revealed that the body was that of Sidney Leslie Goodwin (see page 9), born in September 1910 in Melksham, Wiltshire, England. Sidney was the youngest of six children of Fred and Augusta Goodwin, all of whom were on board. Neither of Sidney's parents nor his other siblings' bodies were ever recovered.

ABOVE The grave of Sidney Goodwin, the 'unknown child' whose identity was discovered in 2007.

LEFT The *Titanic* section of Fairview Lawn Cemetery in Halifax, Nova Scotia.

FINDING TITANIC

DESPITE MANY efforts and attempts, Titanic remained undiscovered for close on 75 years. Until the 1980s the technology to search deep in the ocean did not exist. The cold war and the need to track and investigate sunken submarines were to provide a reason for researching deep ocean exploration.

On 1 September 1985, after a long search and with the aid of remote-controlled vehicles, Titanic was found by Robert Ballard of the Woods Hole Institute, Massachusetts. Titanic lay 2 miles (3km) down, broken in two and slowly decaying.

The search for her had not been easy but the results from the surveys cast new light on the ship, and revived interest in her and the fate of her passengers and crew.

Over the years many artefacts have been recovered: glasses, a top hat, the bell that Fred Fleet rang to attract attention to the iceberg, perfume bottles, spectacles, crockery with the White Star Line logo, jewellery, watches, signage, shoes, letters, menus, even ticket stubs – and much more. There have been touring exhibitions of these items but there is an ongoing legal dispute about who owns both the wreck and the artefacts recovered from it.

BELOW At a press conference at the Woods Hole Institute, Robert Ballard discusses his discovery of the wreck of *Titanic*.

TIME STOOD STILL

Amongst many poignant artefacts recovered from *Titanic* is this pocket watch that belonged to Second Class passenger John Gill, a 24-year-old chauffer from Bristol. His watch stopped at 3.20 a.m.; the ship had sunk at around 2.20 a.m. but, having just crossed the International Date Line, the timepiece was one hour fast. Such personal items are a reminder that what happened that day was a deeply moving and personal tragedy that shocked the world and affected many individuals and families.

RIGHT Waiting for a meal that will never be served – rows of dishes lie amongst the debris of *Titanic* at the bottom of the Atlantic.

THEORIES AND DESTINIES

A CURIOUS FOOTNOTE to *Titanic*'s story comes in a premonition of the disaster from as early as 1898. In a short story entitled 'Futility', Morgan Robertson wrote about a disaster to a liner called *Titan*. The similarities with *Titanic* are uncanny:

TITAN	*TITANIC*
British built	British built
800 feet (244m) long	882 feet (268m) long
Space for 3,000 passengers and crew: 2,000 on board	Space for 3,000 passengers and crew: *c*.2,204 on board
24 lifeboats with capacity for 500 people	20 lifeboats with capacity for 1,178 people
Disaster occurred in April	Disaster occurred in April
Hit iceberg on starboard side	Hit iceberg on starboard side
Travelling at 24–25 knots	Travelling at 22.5 knots

There is also an ingenious conspiracy theory, put forward by Robin Gardiner and Dan van der Vat. In their book *The Riddle of the Titanic* the authors suggest that just before *Titanic* left Belfast for her maiden voyage she was switched with one of her sisters. *Olympic* was also in Belfast, undergoing costly repairs following her collision (whilst under the command of Captain Smith) with British warship HMS *Hawke* off the Isle of Wight. The contention is that as part of an insurance scam *Olympic* took *Titanic*'s name and place and sailed on as *Titanic*. Captain Smith was ordered to engineer an accident on what was now *Titanic* (but had been *Olympic*). The further argument is that Smith hit an iceberg accidentally whilst in the course of the deception.

If the ship that sank really was *Titanic* then what of her contemporaries?

- *Olympic* sailed on until the 1930s as a much-loved liner. She even rammed and sank a U-boat in the First World War.

- *Britannic* never sailed commercially; she was converted to a hospital ship and in 1916 she struck a mine and sank in the Aegean Sea.
- *Lusitania* was sunk by a torpedo fired from a German U-20 submarine off the coast of Ireland in 1915, with the loss of 1,198 lives.
- *Mauretania* held the record for the fastest transatlantic crossing until 1928 and was broken up in the 1930s.

The *Titanic* disaster was the beginning of the end of the Morgan empire. White Star soldiered on until the 1930s when it merged with Cunard as part of a government deal to subsidize the *Queen Mary*, some of the steel for which had been intended for a new White Star liner, *Oceanic*. Cunard White Star is now the Cunard cruise company, part of the US Carnival Group and thus the 150,000 GRT *Queen Mary 2* has an ancestral link to *Titanic*.

J. Bruce Ismay kept out of the public eye for most of the remainder of his life. He retired from active affairs in the mid-1920s, and settled with his wife in Ireland. His health declined in the 1930s due to diabetes and he lost part of his right leg. He returned to England, settling in a small house, and lived until 1937.

BELOW After *Olympic*'s collision with HMS *Hawke* she returned to Belfast, and for a brief time she and the nearly complete *Titanic* were reunited. *Titanic* and *Olympic* are seen together here for the last time, 3 February 1912.

FILMS, FACTS AND FICTION

THE 1997 *TITANIC* movie is well known but there have been many others about the ship – and even a musical. *Titanic the Musical* opened on Broadway in 1997 and won five Tony Awards, including one for Best Musical.

Arguably the best film made about *Titanic* is the 1958 movie *A Night to Remember*, starring Kenneth More as Second Officer Charles Lightoller and David McCallum as radio operator Harold Bride.

The Unsinkable Molly Brown was a 1964 film adaptation of an earlier Broadway musical. Debbie Reynolds starred in the title role of the film, with Marilu Henner taking over for a TV mini-series and Kathy Bates playing the role in the 1997 *Titanic* movie.

Raise the Titanic was a film based on the 1976 novel of the same name by Clive Cussler, telling the fictional story of efforts to bring the remains of the ocean liner to the surface. One of the financiers of the 1980 film is reported to have said that 'it would have been cheaper to lower the Atlantic'.

S.O.S. Titanic was a 1979 movie made for television starring David Janssen as John Jacob Astor and Cloris Leachman as Margaret 'Molly' Brown.

In reality, 1997's *Titanic* is simply another version of *West Side Story* and *Porgy and Bess*, in turn derived from *Romeo and Juliet*. The award-winning *Titanic* blockbuster is an American romance/disaster movie starring Leonardo DiCaprio as Jack Dawson and Kate Winslet as Rose DeWitt Bukater, members of different social classes who fall in love aboard the ship during its ill-fated maiden voyage. Though the central roles and love story are fictitious, some characters are based on historical figures. The film's plot involving a jewel, the Heart of the Ocean, is also fictitious; there was no such treasure on board.

Titanic premiered on 1 November 1997 at the Tokyo International Film Festival to mixed reviews. It is renowned for containing some notable inaccuracies: smoke coming out of the fourth funnel; Jack and Rose, in evening dress, running through the engine areas which in reality would have been full of heat, smoke and coal dust. In addition, passengers could not access the bow of *Titanic* and in 1912 no Third Class passenger would have been allowed in First Class, even if invited. The set designers made the staircase 1½ times the size of the original – apparently it looked better bigger! However, the film won 11 Oscars and for 12 years held the record for being the highest gross-earning film.

BELOW Poster for the 1997 film. Harland and Wolff provided blueprints from their archives to enable the film-makers to build their reconstruction of *Titanic* as accurately as possible.

NOTHING ON EARTH COULD COME BETWEEN THEM.

LEONARDO DiCAPRIO   KATE WINSLET

TITANIC

JOSEPH AND ROSA

As in the 1997 film, there was a J. Dawson on board *Titanic* – but not Jack. Joseph Dawson was a trimmer in the engine room and the 23-year-old's grave is in Fairview Lawn Cemetery, Halifax. The name of the film character was taken from the headstone on which Joseph is remembered as J. Dawson. In addition, while there was no one named Rose in First Class in real life, there was a Rosa on board. Rhoda Mary ('Rosa') Abbott, originally from Aylesbury in Buckinghamshire, England, was travelling in Third Class with her sons, Ross (16) and Eugene (14). Rosa refused to leave the boys and all three were hurled into the waves when *Titanic* sank. Rosa was dragged into a lifeboat; Ross's body was recovered; Eugene's was not. Rosa lived until she was 73, but never recovered from her ordeal, physically or emotionally.

THE STORY CONTINUES

A CENTURY LATER, the story of *Titanic* continues to fascinate. The simplest of artefacts – for example postcards and photographs – can fetch thousands of pounds at auction.

Research into the disaster continues, and with ever-increasingly sophisticated technology the results give us more theories as to what happened that fateful night.

Recent evidence suggests that the long time lag between the collision and the launching of the first lifeboat – over an hour – could have been because those in charge believed the ship would sink more slowly. *Titanic* had an expansion joint between the third and fourth funnel (like the joints on bridges that allow for expansion in hot weather). Compared with the joint built into *Britannic* after the disaster, *Titanic*'s was a crude design. It is conjectured by some that this joint could have failed, causing the ship to break up before sinking. Although the US and British inquiries said the ship sank at a sharp angle, the evidence from the wreck suggests a shallower angle and the fact that the stern is some distance from the rest of the wreckage gives credence to the break-up theory.

The evidence from metal recovered from the wreck suggests that the iron (rather than steel) rivets used in the bow may have broken, allowing the plates to separate and that it was this rather than a gash that opened six compartments up to the sea.

Whatever the cause, *Titanic* remains the most well-known and well-documented shipwreck, and a true tragedy. One or two minutes either way and she would not have hit the iceberg. Such is fate.

ABOVE Embroidered silk evening slippers worn by American journalist Edith Russell during the disaster, which she survived.

LEFT A genuine *Titanic* lifejacket, up for auction at Christies in New York in 2008. It was found by a family in Nova Scotia soon after the disaster.

FURTHER INFORMATION

PLACES TO VISIT

As well as frequent *Titanic* exhibitions that tour the world there are several permanent exhibitions, many of which are listed here.

UK

Titanic Museum in Southampton will be a brand new interactive museum, due to open in 2012 in the city's former magistrates' court, next to the Civic Centre.

Maritime Museum in Southampton houses an exhibition devoted to the crew of *Titanic*.
*   The Wool House, Town Quay Road, Southampton SO14 2AR; 023 8022 3941; www.southampton.gov. uk/s-leisure/artsheritage/museums-galleries/maritimemuseum.aspx

Merseyside Maritime Museum in Liverpool has a *Titanic* display.
*   Albert Dock, Liverpool L3 4AQ; 0151 478 4499; www.liverpoolmuseums. org.uk/maritime

Titanic's Dock and Pump House at the Harland and Wolff yard in Belfast is an on-site museum in an area under redevelopment as the Titanic Quarter.
*   NI Science Park, Queen's Road, Belfast BT3 9DT; 028 9073 7813; www.titanicsdock.com

Nomadic is close to Titanic's Dock and Pump House, and is the tender that was based at Cherbourg to bring Second and Third Class passengers out to *Titanic*. Built by Harland and Wolff she was bought at auction in Paris in 2006 for preservation in Belfast.
*   Hamilton Dock, Queens Road, Belfast BT3 9DT; www.nomadicpreservationsociety.co.uk

Ulster Folk and Transport Museum, just outside Belfast, is home to the largest collection of *Titanic* artefacts and information.
*   Cultra, Holywood, Belfast BT18 0EU; 028 9042 8428; www.nmni.com/titanic/Home.aspx

Titanic Quarter is a long-term project under development on Queen's Island in Belfast. When completed it will provide a mixed-use facility including housing, offices, a museum, event space, hotels and other leisure and tourism facilities on this 185 acre (75ha) site.
*   www.titanic-quarter.com

CANADA AND USA

Maritime Museum of the Atlantic has a good *Titanic* collection.
*   1675 Lower Water Street, Halifax, Nova Scotia, Canada, B3J 1S3; 001 902 424 7490; http://museum.gov.ns.ca/mmanew

Fairview Lawn Cemetery, **Mount Olivet Cemetery** and **Baron de Hirsch Cemetery** are all in Halifax and available to visit.

The Titanic Museum is a family-run museum in Massachusetts, and has the Titanic Historical Society's collection of *Titanic* artefacts.
*   208 Main Street, Indian Orchard, Massachusetts; (413) 543 4770; www.titanichistoricalsociety.org/museum

Titanic the Experience in Orlando has re-creations of rooms in the ship, and storytellers in period dress; you can even attend a *Titanic* dinner.
*   7324 International Drive, Orlando, Florida 32819; 407 248-1166; http://titanictheexperience.com

ABOVE Plaque on the former White Star Line offices in Southampton.

ABOVE RIGHT Detail from a *Titanic* memorial in Cobh.

MEMORIALS

Scores of British towns and cities – including Belfast, Southampton, Liverpool, Lichfield (Staffordshire), Colne (Lancashire) – and others around the world have memorials to those who died, especially crew members.

At Cobh (Queenstown) in County Cork (*Titanic*'s last port of call) are memorials to the victims of *Titanic* and *Lusitania*, situated on adjacent street corners, plus one at the railway station, dedicated to emigrants. These can be seen on the 'Titanic Trail', which is a walking tour of the port and town (www.titanic-trail.com).

In the USA, New York's Macy's department store has a memorial to Isidor and Ida Straus; also in New York is the Titanic Memorial Lighthouse. A memorial in Washington DC honours the men who 'gave their lives that women and children might be saved'.

ONLINE

www.encyclopedia-titanica.org is a website dedicated to the history of the ship, passengers and crew.

www.titanic-titanic.com has lots of information and statistics about *Titanic*, her sister ships and the White Star Line.

www.titanicinquiry.org details the American and British inquiries into the disaster.

www.onlinetitanicmuseum.com is a virtual display of a private collection of *Titanic* artefacts and memorabilia.